Thoughts
for
Women:
Joy

© 2014 by Barbour Publishing, Inc.

Written and compiled by Alyssa Fikse.

Print ISBN 978-1-62416-987-8

eBook Editions:
Adobe Digital Edition (.epub) 978-1-63058-011-7
Kindle and MobiPocket Edition (.prc) 978-1-63058-012-4

Published by Barbour Books, an imprint of Barbour Publishing, Inc., P.O. Box 719, Uhrichsville, Ohio 44683, www.barbourbooks.com

Our mission is to publish and distribute inspirational products offering exceptional value and biblical encouragement to the masses.

Printed in the United States of America.

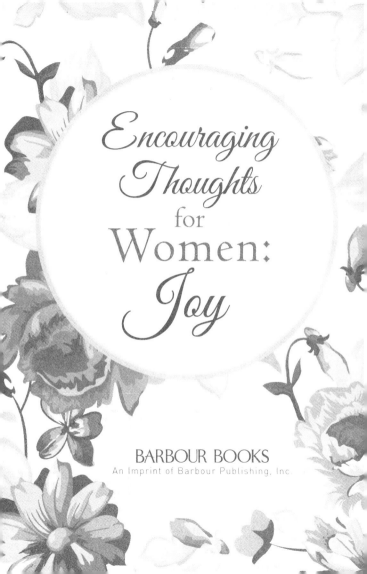

Encouraging Thoughts for Women: Joy

BARBOUR BOOKS

An Imprint of Barbour Publishing, Inc.

Contents

Introduction

*L*et's face it: it's not easy being a woman. Women are expected to juggle jobs, manage the house, and take care of their families, and they are supposed to do it in heels. The pressure of being a woman can often be discouraging, and it is easy to get bogged down. However, you are beloved by the Father no matter how "successful" you are in having it all, and that is cause for joy. In fact, there are many reasons for Christians to be joyful, but some are less obvious than others. Through examining the Word of God, it soon becomes clear that joy is an integral part of the Christian life.

JOY *in Salvation*

But now, thus says the LORD, who created you,
O Jacob, and He who formed you, O Israel: "Fear not,
for I have redeemed you; I have called you by your name;
you are Mine. When You pass through the waters, I will be
with you; and through the rivers, they shall not overflow
you. When you walk through the fire, you shall not
be burned, nor shall the flame scorch you."
ISAIAH 43:1–2 NKJV

*R*ejection is a painful and powerful thing. It comes in many forms, from the clique that froze you out in middle school to the employer who thought that you "just weren't the right fit for the company." If we derive our worth from earthly things, every day can bring disappointment upon disappointment. It can seem impossible to measure up. It is so easy to sink deeper and deeper into despair, until it feels like you are drowning beneath inadequacy and a world that doesn't give you a minute to catch your breath.

That is the moment when God finds you. Sometimes you are at the end of your rope, crying out for help in the darkness. Sometimes you are dragged unwillingly into the light. Either way, our Father is there to welcome you with open arms. Isaiah 43 says, "I have called you by your name; you are Mine." You are His. You are a child of the Creator, Redeemer, and Sustainer of all things. You are valued by Him, not because of what you do, but because of who you are: His.

There is so much joy to be gleaned from living under the salvation of Christ. You can now move ahead with confidence that you are loved and valued. Your worth is now found in Christ, and there is nothing in your life that He cannot handle. You are no longer alone, and that is cause for joy.

But let all who take refuge in you rejoice;
let them ever sing for joy,
and spread your protection over them,
that those who love your name may exult in you.
PSALM 5:11 ESV

Restore to me the joy of Your salvation,
and uphold me by Your generous Spirit.
PSALM 51:12 NKJV

The LORD is my strength and song,
and He has become my salvation;
He is my God, and I will praise Him;
my father's God, and I will exalt Him.
EXODUS 15:2 NKJV

All joy emphasizes our pilgrim status;
always reminds, beckons, awakens desire.
Our best havings are wantings.

C. S. LEWIS

It is the consciousness of the threefold
joy of the Lord, His joy in ransoming us,
His joy in dwelling within us as our
Savior and Power for the fruitbearing,
and His joy in possessing us, as His Bride
and His delight; it is the consciousness
of this joy which is our real strength.
Our joy in Him may be a fluctuating thing:
His joy in us knows no change.

HUDSON TAYLOR

Wells of Salvation

With joy you will drink deeply
from the fountain of salvation!
ISAIAH 12:3 NLT

In biblical times, women would go to the local
well for water. They would drop the bucket down,
down, down, then lift it up, filled to the brim.
Today, the Lord wants you to reach down into
His well of salvation and, with great joy, draw
up the bucket. Remember how He saved you?
Delivered you? Remember His grace?
Is your bucket filled to the brim? If so,
then that's something to celebrate!

Dear Lord, thank You for the joy of Your salvation! You have taken my downtrodden spirit and given me a new purpose through Your will. You have taken my weeping and turned it into laughing. You have taken my fear and turned it into delight. I know that I am a child of God and that my value is in You. I cannot boast in my accomplishments; my joy is all through the work that Christ has done in me. Amen.

"The LORD lives! Blessed be my Rock!
Let God be exalted, the Rock of my salvation!"
2 SAMUEL 22:47 NKJV

"And now arise, O LORD God,
and go to your resting place,
you and the ark of your might.
Let your priests, O LORD God,
be clothed with salvation,
and let your saints rejoice in your goodness."
2 CHRONICLES 6:41 ESV

Salvation belongs to the LORD.
Your blessing is upon Your people.
PSALM 3:8 NKJV

But I have trusted in Your mercy;
my heart shall rejoice in Your salvation.
PSALM 13:5 NKJV

You have turned my mourning into dancing;
you have taken off my sackcloth and clothed me with joy,
so that my soul may praise you and not be silent.
O LORD my God, I will give thanks to you forever.
PSALM 30:11–12 NRSV

Satisfy us in the morning with your unfailing love,
that we may sing for joy and be glad all our days.
PSALM 90:14 NIV

Never be lacking in zeal, but keep your
spiritual fervor, serving the Lord. Be joyful in hope,
patient in affliction, faithful in prayer.
ROMANS 12:11–12 NIV

The Rock of Our Salvation

O come, let us sing unto the LORD:
let us make a joyful noise to
the rock of our salvation.

PSALM 95:1 KJV

God never changes. He's the same—
yesterday, today, and forever. We go through
a multitude of changes in our lives, but,
praise God, He's consistent. Doesn't that
bring joy to your heart, to realize that the
Creator of the universe is our Rock? And don't
you feel like celebrating when you realize
that, no matter how much you mess up,
His promise of salvation is true?
Praise be to the Lord, our Rock!

Dear Lord, You are ever constant.
Though the world changes around me
and I am swept away, You are always
there to bring me back to Your side.
Even when I wander away, You are always
there to gently guide me back. Thank You,
Father, for Your constant and unfailing love.
I rejoice in Your presence, and I look
forward to doing so forever. Amen.

What think we of Christ? Is He altogether
glorious in our eyes, and precious to our hearts?
May Christ be our joy, our confidence, our all.
May we be daily made more like Him,
and more devoted to His service.

MATTHEW HENRY

How divinely full of glory and pleasure
shall that hour be when all the millions of
mankind that have been redeemed by the blood
of the Lamb of God shall meet together and
stand around Him, with every tongue and every
heart full of joy and praise! How astonishing will
be the glory and the joy of that day when all the
saints shall join together in one common song of
gratitude and love, and everlasting thankfulness to
this Redeemer! With that unknown delight, and
inexpressible satisfaction, shall all that are saved
from the ruins of sin and hell address the Lamb
that was slain, and rejoice in His presence!

ISAAC WATTS

JOY *in Heaven*

*"He will wipe away every tear from their eyes,
and death shall be no more, neither shall there
be mourning, nor crying, nor pain anymore,
for the former things have passed away."*

REVELATION 21:4 ESV

The world is in chaos. Wars rage, people are brutalized daily, and it seems like new diseases emerge out of nowhere. Closer to home, your friends and family lie to you, your car breaks down at the worst possible moment, and the bills pile up. When you look at the world around you, despair seems like the only possible response. Feelings of hopelessness can paralyze you, and sometimes you wonder, What is the point in even trying? The powers of sin seem to be too strong. This can't be all that there is.

Fortunately for the believer, this isn't it. This world is only the first step in our journey. Christians are encouraged that true joy is found in heaven. All of the fleeting happiness found on earth is just a faint reflection of what awaits you in heaven. When you finally reach the end of the road and rejoin the Father in heaven, your joy will be complete. In heaven there is no pain, no suffering, and no sin. You will no longer be rejoicing about what is to come; the ultimate joy, being in the presence of God, will be yours! When you feel the bitter anguish that comes with life on earth, remember that the Lord has promised you an eternal life in heaven. What a beautiful day that will be!

Then I saw a new heaven and a new earth, for the first heaven and the first earth had passed away, and the sea was no more. And I saw the holy city, new Jerusalem, coming down out of heaven from God, prepared as a bride adorned for her husband. And I heard a loud voice from the throne saying, "Behold, the dwelling place of God is with man. He will dwell with them, and they will be his people, and God himself will be with them as their God. He will wipe away every tear from their eyes, and death shall be no more, neither shall there be mourning, nor crying, nor pain anymore, for the former things have passed away." And he who was seated on the throne said, "Behold, I am making all things new." Also he said, "Write this down, for these words are trustworthy and true."

REVELATION 21:1–5 ESV

If I find in myself desires which nothing in this
world can satisfy, the only logical explanation
is that I was made for another world.

C. S. LEWIS

The joy of Christ and the joy of the world cannot
consist together. A heart delighted with worldly
joy cannot feel the consolations of the Spirit; the
one of these destroys the other; but in sanctified
trouble, the comforts of God's Word are felt and
perceived in a most sensible manner.

ABRAHAM WRIGHT

Eternal Joy!

And the ransomed of the LORD shall return, and come to Zion
with songs and everlasting joy upon their heads: they shall
obtain joy and gladness, and sorrow and sighing shall flee away.

ISAIAH 35:10 KJV

Have you ever pondered eternity? Forever and
ever and ever. . . ? Our finite minds can't grasp
the concept, and yet one thing we understand
from scripture: we will enter eternity in a state
of everlasting joy and gladness. No more tears!
No sorrow! An eternal joy-fest awaits us!
Now that's something to celebrate!

Dear Lord, thank You for the promise of
heaven! I long for the day when I will be in
Your presence for eternity! What a beautiful
thing that will be. Keep me focused on heaven,
but remind me to stay present during my time on
earth as well. Help me be a light to those around me,
always pointing them toward You with my joy. Amen.

*But as it is, they desire a better country, that is,
a heavenly one. Therefore God is not ashamed to be
called their God, for he has prepared for them a city.*
HEBREWS 11:16 ESV

*"I give them eternal life, and they will never perish,
and no one will snatch them out of my hand."*
JOHN 10:28 ESV

*"Fear not, little flock, for it is your Father's
good pleasure to give you the kingdom."*
LUKE 12:32 ESV

*[Give] thanks to the Father, who has qualified you
to share in the inheritance of the saints in light.*
COLOSSIANS 1:12 ESV

"It was fitting to celebrate and be glad, for this your brother was dead, and is alive; he was lost, and is found."
LUKE 15:32 ESV

"Nevertheless, do not rejoice in this, that the spirits are subject to you, but rejoice that your names are written in heaven."
LUKE 10:20 ESV

Therefore let us be grateful for receiving a kingdom that cannot be shaken, and thus let us offer to God acceptable worship, with reverence and awe, for our God is a consuming fire.
HEBREWS 12:28–29 ESV

Enter into the Joy

His lord said unto him, Well done, thou good and faithful servant: thou hast been faithful over a few things, I will make thee ruler over many things: enter thou into the joy of thy lord.

MATTHEW 25:21 KJV

When you think of standing before the Lord face-to-face, are you overwhelmed with fear or awestruck with great joy? Oh, what a glorious day it will be when we hear Him speak those words, "Well done, thou good and faithful servant." When He ushers us into the joy of His presence for all eternity, our fears and hesitations will be forever washed away. Spend time in joyous rehearsal today!

Dear Lord, I place my hope in You! You are faithful, and You keep Your promises. I cannot wait to be in Your immediate presence and to be united with the entire body of believers in heaven. That will be a joyous day, and I cannot wait to raise my voice in praise with the saints! I may be bound to this earth for the time being, but I continue to long for heaven. Amen.

Begin to rejoice in the Lord, and your bones will flourish like an herb, and your cheeks will glow with the bloom of health and freshness. Worry, fear, distrust, care—all are poisonous! Joy is balm and healing, and if you will but rejoice, God will give you power.

A. B. SIMPSON

The only lasting and fully satisfying joys for any man lie on the other side of the cross.

WALTER J. CHANTRY

JOY *in Obedience*

The precepts of the LORD are right, giving joy to the heart.
The commands of the LORD are radiant, giving light to the eyes.
PSALM 19:8 NIV

*H*uman beings are willful creatures from the day they are born. One of the first things children learn is to say "No!" You are born fighting for control of your own life, and the struggle for independence continues for the rest of your life. However, a relationship with Jesus sheds some light on matters of the heart: left to their own devices, people tend toward sin and self-destruction. Only through obedience to Christ are salvation and true joy found.

Obedience is a difficult thing, but to follow Christ means freedom from sin. He only wants what is best for us, and that requires obeying His rules. There is always a measure of grace, but the process of sanctification is often difficult. Breaking fleshly, sinful habits can be painful and can seem impossible. However, Jesus will be there every step of the way, beckoning you to leave behind the old self and take up the new. Scriptures tell us that living a life of obedience will lead to a life of prosperity, so what do you have to lose?

As you draw closer to the heart of Jesus, obedience to Christ will actually be the source of your joy! The world teaches us to put our own interests first, but surrendering to the will of God and living our lives in obedience leads to a more fulfilling, and therefore joyful, life.

You will show me the path of life; in Your presence is fullness
of joy; at Your right hand are pleasures forevermore.
PSALM 16:11 NKJV

The prospect of the righteous is joy,
but the hopes of the wicked come to nothing.
PROVERBS 10:28 NIV

For this is the love of God, that we keep his commandments.
And his commandments are not burdensome.
1 JOHN 5:3 ESV

Praise the LORD! Blessed is the man who fears
the LORD, who greatly delights in his commandments!
PSALM 112:1 ESV

The reward of being "faithful over a few things" is just the same as being "faithful over many things"; for the emphasis falls upon the same word; it is the faithful who will enter "into the joy of their Lord."

CHARLES S. ROBINSON

Let a man begin with an earnest "I ought," and if he perseveres, by God's grace he will end in the free blessedness of "I will." Let him force himself to abound in small acts of duty, and he will, by and by, find them the joyous habit of his soul.

FREDERICK W. ROBERTSON

Joyful Obedience

Now unto him that is able to keep you from
falling, and to present you faultless before
the presence of his glory with exceeding joy. . .
JUDE 24 KJV

Our obedience makes God happy and should
make us happy, too. In fact, the more difficult it
is to obey, the more joyful we should be. Why?
Because a big situation calls for a big God. And
our God is bigger than anything we could ask or
think. He alone can prevent us from falling. So
if you're struggling in the area of obedience,
surrender your will. Enter into joyful obedience.

Dear Lord, so often I fail in keeping Your commands. I think only of myself and my own appetites. Remind me of Your words and Your commands. Help me to burn Your law onto my heart and surrender myself to Your will. Thank You for Your loving-kindness and blessings! Make my heart desire You in everything, and make my joy more complete. Amen.

"Yet I do not seek my own glory; there is one who seeks it and he is the judge. Very truly, I tell you, whoever keeps my word will never see death."

JOHN 8:50–51 NRSV

"If you keep my commandments, you will abide in my love, just as I have kept my Father's commandments and abide in his love. These things I have spoken to you, that my joy may be in you, and that your joy may be full. This is my commandment, that you love one another as I have loved you."

JOHN 15:10–12 ESV

*And he said to him, "Why do you ask me about
what is good? There is only one who is good.
If you would enter life, keep the commandments."*
MATTHEW 19:17 ESV

*The wise of heart will receive commandments,
but a babbling fool will come to ruin.*
PROVERBS 10:8 ESV

*I incline my heart to perform
your statutes forever, to the end.*
PSALM 119:112 ESV

*"If you know these things,
blessed are you if you do them."*
JOHN 13:17 ESV

Uprightness

"I know also, my God, that You test the heart and have pleasure in uprightness."

I Chronicles 29:17 NKJV

Everyone wants to be happy, right? We know that our obedience to the Lord results in a life of great joy. But our obedience does something else, too. It brings pleasure to our heavenly Father. When we live uprightly, God is pleased. Today, instead of focusing on your own happiness, give some thought to putting a smile on *His* face.

Dear Lord, You loved me first, and I want to honor You. So often I think only of my own happiness, but I want to change that and live for You and Your glory every day. Change my hardened heart and replace it with one that is molded into Your image. I no longer want to live just for myself. Help me to obey and to chase after You every day of my life. Thank You for guiding me toward joy with a patient hand. Amen.

Be good, keep your feet dry, your eyes open, your heart at peace, and your soul in the joy of Christ.

THOMAS MERTON

The world looks for happiness through self-assertion. The Christian knows that joy is found in self-abandonment. "If a man will let himself be lost for My sake," Jesus said, "he will find his true self."

ELISABETH ELLIOT

The Lord gives his people perpetual joy when they walk in obedience to Him.

D. L. MOODY

Holy joy will be the oil to the wheels of our obedience.

MATTHEW HENRY

JOY *in Gratitude*

How can we thank God enough for you in return for all the joy we have in the presence of our God because of you?

I THESSALONIANS 3:9 NIV

When you consider all that the Lord has done for you, it is simply impossible not to be grateful. People are truly wretched creatures, slaves to their sin. Even so, Jesus came to earth and died so that their relationships with the Father can be restored. You did nothing to deserve that sacrifice, and yet Jesus still did it! What a cause for joy and gratitude!

If you are to be truly grateful for the sacrifice that Jesus made, joy should permeate every single aspect of your life. You were literally plucked from the jaws of hell and restored to a place in heaven.

Hallelujah! God is good! This thankfulness should permeate every aspect of your life—don't keep quiet! Spread your joy! The childhood song says, "This little light of mine, I'm gonna let it shine." Let your gratitude shine!

Overflowing of this joy should show in how you interact with others. You have been saved, so share this good news. Help others discover what Jesus did for them as well. Helping lead others heavenward will only increase your joy. Your testimony could have a very important impact on those around you. Make His wonderful deeds known! Your very status as an image bearer should make you grateful—God loved you so much that He crafted you in *His* image.

Let the peace of Christ rule in your hearts, since as members of one body you were called to peace. And be thankful. Let the message of Christ dwell among you richly as you teach and admonish one another with all wisdom through psalms, hymns, and songs from the Spirit, singing to God with gratitude in your hearts.

COLOSSIANS 3:15–16 NIV

So then, just as you received Christ Jesus as Lord, continue to live your lives in him, rooted and built up in him, strengthened in the faith as you were taught, and overflowing with thankfulness.

COLOSSIANS 2:6–7 NIV

The very nature of joy makes nonsense of our
common distinction between having and wanting.

C. S. LEWIS

Gratitude changes the pangs
of memory into a tranquil joy.

DIETRICH BONHOEFFER

Joy is the simplest form of gratitude.

KARL BARTH

There is a joy which is not given to the ungodly,
but to those who love Thee for Thine own sake,
whose joy Thou Thyself art. And this is the happy
life, to rejoice to Thee, of Thee, for Thee;
this it is, and there is no other.

SAINT AUGUSTINE

A Joyful Noise

Make a joyful noise unto the LORD, all ye lands.
PSALM 100:1 KJV

How do we praise God for His many blessings?
If we follow the pattern of Old Testament
saints, then we lift our voices in thanksgiving!
We let others know. With a resounding voice,
we echo our praises, giving thanks for all He has
done and all He continues to do. So praise
Him today! Make a joyful noise!

Dear Lord, You shower me with blessings every day! Thank You for Your faithful provision in every aspect of my life. You meet my needs, and still Your blessings overflow. I never want to take Your graciousness for granted. I want to shout Your glory from the mountaintops! You have blessed me beyond measure! Thank You for multiplying my cause for joy. Amen.

Through the victories you gave, his glory is great;
you have bestowed on him splendor and majesty.
Surely you have granted him unending blessings and
made him glad with the joy of your presence. For the
king trusts in the Lord; *through the unfailing love*
of the Most High he will not be shaken.

Psalm 21:5–7 niv

But thanks be to God, who always leads us as captives
in Christ's triumphal procession and uses us to spread
the aroma of the knowledge of him everywhere.

2 Corinthians 2:14 niv

Give thanks unto the LORD, call upon his name,
make known his deeds among the people.
1 CHRONICLES 16:8 KJV

He redeemed us in order that the blessing given to
Abraham might come to the Gentiles through Christ Jesus,
so that by faith we might receive the promise of the Spirit.
GALATIANS 3:14 NIV

They will receive blessing from the LORD
and vindication from God their Savior.
PSALM 24:5 NIV

Abounding with Blessings

A faithful man shall abound with blessings.
PROVERBS 28:20 KJV

To *abound* means to have more than enough. When
you're abounding, all of your needs are met. . .
and then some! How wonderful to go through
such seasons. So what do we have to do to qualify
for these "more than enough" blessings? Only
one thing: be found faithful. Trust God during
the lean seasons. Don't give up! Then, when the
"abounding" seasons come, you can truly rejoice!

Dear Lord, I know that You always provide for me, even in the moments when it seems that my needs are not being met. You know what I need, and You always provide in one way or another. I need to learn to trust You in *every* situation, not just when things are going my way. Deepen my faith. Help me to find joy in every circumstance. Amen.

He that hath so many and great causes of joy, yet
is in love with sorrow and peevishness, deserves to
starve in the midst of plenty, and to want comfort,
while he is encircled with blessings.

JEREMY TAYLOR

Like supernatural effervescence, praise will
sometimes bubble up from the joy of simply
knowing Christ. Praise like that is. . .delight.
Pure pleasure! But praise can also be supernatural
determination. A decisive action. Praise like that is
. . .quiet resolve. Fixed devotion. Strength of spirit.

JONI EARECKSON TADA

Joy *in Forgiveness*

Be kind to each other, tenderhearted, forgiving one another,
just as God through Christ has forgiven you.
EPHESIANS 4:32 NLT

❦

Imagine you are stuck in a cell. It isn't your
fault that you have been put there—the unkindness
and neglect of others landed you in that prison.
However, you are holding the key in your hand. You
have the power to leave that cell, but it will require
some effort and some pain. Would you use your
key to leave?

Forgiveness is similar to that cell: someone has
wronged you, and you are both crippled because of
it. The healing process can be yours if you choose to
forgive others, but it isn't always easy. People often

opt to hold on to their grudges at the expense of their joy. A lack of forgiveness is truly damaging to the heart. Clinging to past hurts keeps the wound fresh and open, unable to heal. However, when you examine the measure of forgiveness that was doled out to you from God, forgiving others seems like the only logical choice.

Living a life of accepting and giving forgiveness is living a life of joy. You have been washed clean, and so have your fellow believers, by receiving and offering forgiveness. In Ephesians 4:32 you are called to be kind and forgive, as God through Christ has forgiven you. Praise Him for His forgiveness and mercy!

*"If you forgive anyone's sins, their sins are forgiven;
if you do not forgive them, they are not forgiven."*
JOHN 20:23 NIV

*"For if you forgive others their trespasses, your heavenly
Father will also forgive you; but if you do not forgive others,
neither will your Father forgive your trespasses."*
MATTHEW 6:14–15 NRSV

*Blessed is he whose transgression
is forgiven, whose sin is covered.*
PSALM 32:1 KJV

After grief for sin there
should be joy for forgiveness.

A. W. PINK

When the heart is full of joy, it always allows
its joy to escape. It is like the fountain in the
marketplace; whenever it is full it runs away in
streams, and so soon as it ceases to overflow, you
may be quite sure that it has ceased to be full.
The only full heart is the overflowing heart.

CHARLES SPURGEON

Forgiveness is the remission of sins. For it is
by this that what has been lost, and was
found, is saved from being lost again.

SAINT AUGUSTINE

"Forgive Us Our Debts"

"Forgive us our debts, as we also have forgiven our debtors."
MATTHEW 6:12 NIV

Is it true that God only forgives us to the extent that we forgive others? That's what the scripture teaches! It's so important not to hold a grudge. It hurts you, and it hurts the one you're refusing to forgive. If you've been holding someone in unforgiveness, may today be the day when you let it go. There is incredible joy in both forgiving and *being* forgiven.

Dear Lord, make me willing to forgive. Help me to move past my anger and my pain, and offer a hand of friendship to those who have wronged me. This anger robs me of my joy. Show me that Your Son was willing to die for the sins of the world, offering Himself up in the ultimate act of forgiveness. I pray that I may learn from His example and spread joy and love instead of sowing dissension. Amen.

*For the sake of your name, L*ORD,
forgive my iniquity, though it is great.
PSALM 25:11 NIV

"For if you forgive other people when they sin against you,
your heavenly Father will also forgive you."
MATTHEW 6:14 NIV

"Do not judge, and you will not be judged.
Do not condemn, and you will not be condemned.
Forgive, and you will be forgiven."
LUKE 6:37 NIV

So watch yourselves. *"If your brother or sister sins against you, rebuke them; and if they repent, forgive them."*

LUKE 17:3 NIV

"Blessed are those whose transgressions are forgiven, whose sins are covered."

ROMANS 4:7 NIV

Bear with each other and forgive one another if any of you has a grievance against someone. Forgive as the Lord forgave you.

COLOSSIANS 3:13 NIV

The Capacity to Forgive

*Then Peter came to him and asked, "Lord, how often should
I forgive someone who sins against me? Seven times?"*
"No, not seven times," Jesus replied, "but seventy times seven!"
MATTHEW 18:21–22 NLT

It's easy to get fed up with people who repeatedly
hurt you and then ask for forgiveness. We grow
weary with their promise that they won't do it
again. If someone has repeatedly hurt you, ask the
Lord to give you wisdom regarding the relationship,
then ask Him to give you the capacity to forgive,
even when it seems impossible. Surely joy will rise
up in your soul as you watch God at work.

Dear Lord, help me to forgive myself. I know the sacrifice that was made on my behalf by Jesus, and yet I continue to sin. The guilt keeps me from truly experiencing the joy offered to me. By accepting the forgiveness that is freely offered, I am more able to pick myself up and move on toward joy. Thank You for Your continual forgiveness and for being patient with my feet of clay. Amen.

To love means loving the unlovable. To forgive
means pardoning the unpardonable. Faith means
believing the unbelievable. Hope means hoping
when everything seems hopeless.

G. K. CHESTERTON

Behold, what manner of love is this,
that Christ should be arraigned and we
adorned, that the curse should be laid on
His head and the crown set on ours.

THOMAS WATSON

Our love for God and our appreciation of His
love and forgiveness will be in proportion to the
recognition of our sin and unworthiness.

DAVE HUNT

Joy *in* Worship

Ascribe to the LORD the glory due his name;
bring an offering and come before him.
Worship the LORD in the splendor of his holiness.

I CHRONICLES 16:29 NIV

*E*nglish poet John Donne wrote, "No man is an island, entire of itself; every man is a piece of the continent, a part of the main." Human beings were not meant to be alone, and this is especially true of Christians. Corporate worship with other believers is an essential balm to the heart. There is a certain kind of joy that can only be found when surrounded by Christians praising the name of Jesus. Often, because church is inconvenient or demanding, people opt out, claiming "busyness" or "not finding the right fit." Keep at it, no matter your stage of life.

Communing with other Christians is beneficial to all believers, whether they are single, married with families, or empty nesters. Look for a small group to join; if you can't find one, start one! Finding a more intimate community to be a part of is just as important as being a part of the greater body of Christ.

It might not happen right away. You will feel like you are attending church simply out of duty. After a long week of working and taking care of your family, a morning to sleep in seems like the paramount of luxury. Your alarm sounds. You consider hitting SNOOZE and rolling over. However, something makes you pause. Instead of ignoring it, you wake up and head to church. As soon as the music starts and everyone begins praising in earnest, you will know you made the right choice. This joy found in worshiping with other believers is better than that extra few hours of sleep.

"Surely God does not reject one who is blameless or
strengthen the hands of evildoers. He will yet fill your
mouth with laughter and your lips with shouts of joy."
JOB 8:20–21 NIV

Sing joyfully to the LORD, you righteous;
it is fitting for the upright to praise him.
PSALM 33:1 NIV

Therefore if you have any encouragement from being united
with Christ, if any comfort from his love, if any common
sharing in the Spirit, if any tenderness and compassion,
then make my joy complete by being like-minded,
having the same love, being one in spirit and of one mind.
PHILIPPIANS 2:1–2 NIV

Dear Lord, create in me an open heart. Do not let my worries and the difficulties of modern life create a barrier between me and other believers. Please put people around me who encourage me in my spiritual walk, and also those whom I can in turn encourage. I raise my voice in praise to You, Lord, and I am renewed. Thank You for accepting my feeble accolades. Amen.

I have no greater joy than to hear that
my children are walking in the truth.
3 JOHN 1:4 NIV

Then make my joy complete by being like-minded,
having the same love, being one in spirit and of one mind.
PHILIPPIANS 2:2 NIV

How lovely on the mountains are the feet of
him who brings good news, who announces
peace and brings good news of happiness.
ISAIAH 52:7 NASB

Just as a body, though one, has many parts,
but all its many parts form one body, so it is with Christ.
I CORINTHIANS 12:12 NIV

When large numbers of people share their joy
in common, the happiness of each is greater
because each adds fuel to the other's flame.

We need to discover all over again that worship
is natural to the Christian, as it was to the godly
Israelites who wrote the psalms, and that the habit
of celebrating the greatness and graciousness of God
yields an endless flow of thankfulness, joy, and zeal.

J. I. PACKER

It is His joy that remains in
us that makes our joy full.

A. B. SIMPSON

Lift Up Your Voice!

And at midnight Paul and Silas prayed,
and sang praises unto God: and the prisoners heard them.
ACTS 16:25 KJV

Are you a closet praiser? Happy to worship God in
the privacy of your own home but nervous about
opening up and praising Him in public? Oh, may
this be the day you break through that barrier.
Corporate praise as you come together with your
brothers and sisters in the Lord to worship Him is
powerful! May you come to know the fullness of His
joy as you worship side by side with fellow believers!

Dear Lord, let my enthusiasm for praising You be infectious! I want to be a light to everyone who crosses my path. Let the joy that comes from worshipping with other believers bleed over into every aspect of my life. Whenever I worship with my fellow believers, remind me that even though we are all very different, we are all members of the body of Christ and are therefore unified in our goal and our joy. Amen.

I will declare thy name unto my brethren,
in the midst of the church will I sing praise unto thee.
HEBREWS 2:12 KJV

Ascribe to the LORD the glory due his name;
worship the LORD in the splendor of his holiness.
PSALM 29:2 NIV

"God is spirit, and his worshipers must
worship in the Spirit and in truth."
JOHN 4:24 NIV

Above all sing spiritually. Have an eye to God in
every word you sing. Aim at pleasing Him more than
yourself, or any other creature. In order to do this,
attend strictly to the sense of what you sing, and see
that your heart is not carried away with the sound,
but offered to God continually; so shall your singing
be such as the Lord will approve here, and reward
you when He cometh in the clouds of heaven.

JOHN WESLEY

To gather with God's people in united adoration of
the Father is as necessary to the Christian life as prayer.

MARTIN LUTHER

Joy in the Battle

Then they returned, every man of Judah and Jerusalem,
and Jehoshaphat in the forefront of them, to go
again to Jerusalem with joy; for the LORD had
made them to rejoice over their enemies.

2 CHRONICLES 20:27 KJV

Enemy forces were just around the bend.
Jehoshaphat, king of Judah, called his people
together. After much prayer, he sent the
worshippers (the Levites) to the front lines, singing
joyful praises as they went. The battle was won!
When you face your next battle, praise your way
through it! Strength and joy will rise up within you!
Prepare for victory!

Dear Lord, help me to worship You even when it isn't easy. When things are going well, it is easy to be joyful and let that joy be made manifest as praise.

Teach me how to be joyful even in battle, to sing Your praises when my enemies surround me. Thank You for being by my side even when times get tough. I will praise You through the storm. Amen.

As the saints of God meet together, Jesus manifests
Himself. And seeing Him, there comes to us a
new joy and peace, a new sense of purpose and
worthfulness of life. Seeing Him there comes to
us a new power for battle and for conquest.

CLOVIS G. CHAPPELL

Do not let Sunday be taken from you. If your
soul has no Sunday, it becomes an orphan.

ALBERT SCHWEITZER

When we really worship anything,
we love not only its clearness but its
obscurity. We exult in its very invisibility.

G. K. CHESTERTON

JOY *in Prayer*

I call on you, my God, for you will answer me;
turn your ear to me and hear my prayer.

PSALM 17:6 NIV

❈

*W*omen are in a constant state of noise.
Everywhere you go, there is so much information to
process. You talk to your children. You talk to their
teachers. Your boss gives you the rundown for the
day. Headlines from the covers of magazines all
vie for your attention in the checkout line. There
is a constant stream of information coming from
the Internet, and the television is always on. There
are very few moments of silence and reflection.
While these things can create a rush, and even
cause feelings of euphoria, they do not actually
promote real joy. In the midst of a world constantly
screaming, it is easy to forget that God often speaks
in the still, quiet moments. You just have to turn
your ear to hear.

What a wonderful gift it is that the God of the universe wants to hear from *you!* What a cause for joy! He crafted the mountains and made the rivers flow, but He still cares about the trials and triumphs of your day. For some reason, though, prayer doesn't always come easy. Feelings of inadequacy and fear of judgment often turn many off from the idea of prayer, but that is a truly warped view of prayer. God is waiting with open arms, ready to heal your brokenness and give you joy.

In the book of Acts, we read that the early believers were constantly in prayer, in the good times and the bad. Adopt this model—take a break from the noise and spend some time with the Father.

Hear my prayer, O God;
listen to the words of my mouth.

PSALM 54:2 NIV

O you who answer prayer! To you all flesh shall come. When
deeds of iniquity overwhelm us, you forgive our transgressions.

PSALM 65:2–3 NRSV

Praise be to God, who has not rejected
my prayer or withheld his love from me!

PSALM 66:20 NIV

Dear Lord, thank You for always hearing my prayer. Give me the wisdom to accept Your answer, even if it is no. Father, accept my praise, feeble as it is! Being able to talk with You is a source of constant joy. Guide me on Your path, and help me to always seek Your will. I am confident that my prayers are heard. You are gracious in all things. Amen.

May my prayer be set before you like incense;
may the lifting up of my hands be like the evening sacrifice.
PSALM 141:2 NIV

The LORD is far from the wicked,
but he hears the prayer of the righteous.
PROVERBS 15:29 NIV

They all joined together constantly in prayer, along with the
women and Mary the mother of Jesus, and with his brothers.
ACTS 1:14 NIV

Prayer should be the means by which I, at all times,
receive all that I need, and, for this reason, be my
daily refuge, my daily consolation, my daily joy,
my source of rich and inexhaustible joy in life.

JOHN CHRYSOSTOM

It matters little what form of prayer we adopt
or how many words we use. What matters is the
faith which lays hold on God, knowing that
He knows our needs before we even ask Him.
That is what gives Christian prayer its boundless
confidence and its joyous certainty.

DIETRICH BONHOEFFER

Approaching the
Throne with Joy

*In every prayer of mine I always make my entreaty
and petition for you all with joy (delight).*
PHILIPPIANS 1:4 AMP

Sometimes we approach our prayer time with
God with a list in hand, much like a child at
Christmastime. Other times we approach the Lord
with fear leading the way. "What happens if He
doesn't respond like I hope?" Though we don't need
to come with a Christmas list in hand, we do need
to confidently approach our heavenly Father and
make our requests with joy. He loves us, after all!
So draw near!

Dear Lord, I am sorry that I often treat my prayers like a grocery list. Instead of thankfulness and joy permeating my prayer, I am too caught up in the things that I want. I should know by now that You satisfy the desires of my heart. Thank You for Your patience and Your constant presence in my life. You, O Lord, are my joy. Amen.

"And when you pray, you shall not be like the hypocrites.
For they love to pray standing in the synagogues and on the
corners of the streets, that they may be seen by men. Assuredly,
I say to you, they have their reward. But you, when you pray,
go into your room, and when you have shut your door, pray to
your Father who is in the secret place; and your Father
who sees in secret will reward you openly."

MATTHEW 6:5–6 NKJV

*Be joyful in hope, patient in
affliction, faithful in prayer.*

ROMANS 12:12 NIV

Prayer is the natural and joyous breathing of the
spiritual life by which the heavenly atmosphere
is inhaled and then exhaled in prayer.

ANDREW MURRAY

What can be more excellent than prayer; what is
more profitable to our life; what sweeter to our
souls; what more sublime, in the course of our
whole life, than the practice of prayer!

SAINT AUGUSTINE

Prayer and praise are the oars by which
a man may row his boat into the deep
waters of the knowledge of Christ.

CHARLES SPURGEON

Joy Leads the Way

Then will I go unto the altar of God, unto God my exceeding
joy: yea, upon the harp will I praise thee, O God my God.
PSALM 43:4 KJV

We're instructed to come into the Lord's presence
with a joy-filled heart. . .to praise our way into the
throne room. Perhaps you're not a musician. You
don't own an instrument and only sing in the shower.
Don't let that keep you from approaching the altar
with a song of praise on your lips. Today, let joy lead
the way, and may your praise be glorious!

Dear Lord, although my voice is not beautiful, I raise it in adoration! You are a just and faithful God, and that is reason for praise! Accept my humble offering and multiply my joy. You are the Creator of all things, and yet You still care about the sparrows of the field— and me. You overflow my heart with joy, and praise cannot help but bubble forth. Amen.

Prayer does not mean that I am to bring God down to my thoughts and my purposes, and bend His government according to my foolish, silly, and sometimes sinful notions. Prayer means that I am to be raised up into feeling, into union and design with Him; that I am to enter into His counsel and carry out His purpose fully.

D. L. MOODY

Prayer, like faith, obtains promises, enlarges their operation, and adds to the measure of their results.

E. M. BOUNDS

JOY in Family

Children, obey your parents in the Lord: for this is right. Honor thy father and mother (which is the first commandment with promise), that it may be well with thee, and thou mayest live long on the earth. And, ye fathers, provoke not your children to wrath: but nurture them in the chastening and admonition of the Lord.

EPHESIANS 6:1–4 ASV

One of the ~~greatest~~ blessings is the blessing of family. Even when your children are driving you insane or your parents meddle, family is reason to rejoice. Having a built-in support system in times of trouble and in times of joy is truly one of God's greatest gifts. A truly unique privilege for the Christian is the joy that comes from leading your family on the path of righteousness. Whether it is encouraging and supporting your coworkers or leading your family heavenward, being an example for Christ is your duty. But oh, what a duty! There is no more beautiful thing than seeing those you love follow Christ.

This is not to say that being in a family is easy. They are the people able to deliver the most joy but also can cause the most pain. Constant communication with God and each other helps maintain a healthy family unit. Laugh together! Cry together! Be honest when someone hurts you, but also constantly share your joy. As your family grows and strengthens, so too will your joy. In order to maintain a good relationship with your family members, make sure they are in a good relationship with the Lord. A family that rejoices in the Lord, rejoices in each other.

Now the God of hope fill you with all joy and
peace in believing, that ye may abound in hope,
through the power of the Holy Ghost.

ROMANS 15:13 KJV

I have no greater joy than to hear that
my children are walking in the truth.

3 JOHN 4 NIV

"And there you shall eat before the LORD your God, and you
shall rejoice in all to which you have put your hand, you and
your households, in which the LORD your God has blessed you."

DEUTERONOMY 12:7 NKJV

Dear Lord, thank You for the gift of family, even when being in a family is hard. Help me to be a source of joy, not a source of strife in my family. Even in the trying times, let me be an example of strength and joy to those around me. Help me to look to You and Your Son as an example, not to the world. Thank You for Your perfect love and patience, and help me to have even a fraction of that for others. Amen.

But Ruth replied, "Don't urge me to leave you or to turn back from you. Where you go I will go, and where you stay I will stay. Your people will be my people and your God my God."

RUTH 1:16 NIV

"Honor your father and your mother, so that you may live long in the land the LORD your God is giving you."

EXODUS 20:12 NIV

Listen, my son, to your father's instruction and do not forsake your mother's teaching.

PROVERBS 1:8 NIV

Family education and order are some of
the chief means of grace; if these are duly
maintained, all the means of grace are
likely to prosper and become effectual.

JONATHAN EDWARDS

What you do in your house is worth as much
as if you did it up in heaven for our Lord God.
We should accustom ourselves to think of our
position and work as sacred and well-pleasing to
God, not on account of the position and work,
but on account of the word and faith from which
the obedience and the work flow.

MARTIN LUTHER

The Fruit of the Spirit

But the fruit of the Spirit is love, joy,
peace, longsuffering, gentleness, goodness, faith.
Galatians 5:22 kjv

Want to know how to have the ideal family
environment? Want to see parents living in peace
with the teens, and vice versa? To obtain a joyous
family environment, you've got to have a fruit-bowl
mentality. Dealing with anger? Reach inside the
bowl for peace. Struggling with impatience? Grab
a slice of long-suffering. Having a problem with
depression? Reach for joy. Keep that fruit bowl
close by! It's going to come in handy!

Dear Lord, help me to always reach for joy. Loving others can be hard, but with Your guidance, I can love others just as You loved us first. No matter what my family looks like, I ask for Your blessing. Whether I am single or have a large family, remind me that every family has value. Help us to follow You in every way, so that the joy of salvation bleeds over into every aspect of family life. Amen.

Children are a heritage from the LORD, offspring a reward from him. Like arrows in the hands of a warrior are children born in one's youth. Blessed is the man whose quiver is full of them. They will not be put to shame when they contend with their opponents in court.
PSALM 127:3–5 NIV

The Spirit himself bears witness with our spirit that we are children of God, and if children, then heirs—heirs of God and fellow heirs with Christ, provided we suffer with him in order that we may also be glorified with him.
ROMANS 8:16–17 ESV

Woman was taken out of man; not out of his
head to top him, nor out of his feet to be
trampled underfoot; but out of his side to
be equal to him, under his arm to be protected,
and near his heart to be loved.

MATTHEW HENRY

Charity begins at home,
but it should not end there.

THOMAS FULLER

Let no Christian parents fall into the delusion
that Sunday school is intended to ease them of
their personal duties. The first and most natural
condition of things is for Christian parents to
train up their own children in the nurture and
admonition of the Lord.

CHARLES SPURGEON

But when the fullness of time had come, God sent forth his Son, born of woman, born under the law, to redeem those who were under the law, so that we might receive adoption as sons. And because you are sons, God has sent the Spirit of his Son into our hearts, crying, "Abba! Father!" So you are no longer a slave, but a son, and if a son, then an heir through God.

GALATIANS 4:4–7 ESV

JOY *in Friendship*

Jonathan said to David, "Go in peace, for we have sworn
friendship with each other in the name of the LORD,
saying, 'The LORD is witness between you and me,
and between your descendants and my descendants forever.'"
Then David left, and Jonathan went back to the town.
I SAMUEL 20:42 NIV

$\mathcal{D}$o you remember your first best friend?
Whether it is building a tree house in the backyard
or getting your dolls ready for a fashion show, it is
truly a childhood blessing to have a best friend to
while away the hours with. This joy does not stay in
childhood, however. It is important in every phase
of life to have a friend with whom you can share
your sorrows and your joys.

A true friend brings happiness and honesty to a relationship, and also has their friend's back in times of trouble. One of the greatest friendships in the Bible is that of David and Jonathan. Jonathan's father, King Saul, felt threatened by David, so he called for David's death. Even in the face of trial, Jonathan rejoiced in his friendship with David and stood at David's side through suffering. This is the mark of a true friend.

Are you a true friend to others? Are you so wrapped up in your own desires that you forget to serve those around you? In order to experience the sweet, healing joy of friendship, you need to make sure that you are holding up your end of the bargain. If you do your part and love your friends in a godly way, you will have cause for rejoicing!

Ointment and perfume delight the heart, and the sweetness
of a man's friend gives delight by hearty counsel.
PROVERBS 27:9 NKJV

"I grieve for you, Jonathan my brother;
you were very dear to me. Your love for me was
wonderful, more wonderful than that of women."
2 SAMUEL 1:26 NIV

I cannot even imagine where I would be today
if it were not for that handful of friends who
have given me a heart full of joy. Let's face it,
friends make life a lot more fun.

CHUCK SWINDOLL

Every man rejoices twice when he has a partner of
his joy; a friend shares my sorrow and makes it but
a moiety, but he swells my joy and makes it double.

JEREMY TAYLOR

Show Yourself Friendly

A man that hath friends must shew himself friendly:
and there is a friend that sticketh closer than a brother.
PROVERBS 18:24 KJV

Ever met someone who just seems to have the gift
of friendship? She's a joy to be around and is always
there when you need her. Perhaps you're that kind
of friend to others. Friendship is a privilege, and
we're blessed to have brothers and sisters in Christ.
But not all friendships are easy. Today, ask the Lord
to show you how to "show yourself friendly" in
every situation. Oh, the joy of great relationships!

Dear Lord, help me to be someone who encourages friendships. Instead of sowing discord wherever I go, let me instead be a beacon of joy. Put in my path those I can minister to, and who in turn can minister to me. I want to drink deeply from the well of friendship so that I may know one of the greatest joys this world can afford. Thank You for this wonderful gift. Amen.

The righteous choose their friends carefully,
but the way of the wicked leads them astray.
PROVERBS 12:26 NIV

A friend loves at all times, and a brother
is born for a time of adversity.
PROVERBS 17:17 NIV

One who has unreliable friends soon comes to ruin,
but there is a friend who sticks closer than a brother.
PROVERBS 18:24 NIV

Better is open rebuke than hidden love. Wounds from a friend can be trusted, but an enemy multiplies kisses.
PROVERBS 27:5–6 NIV

Iron sharpens iron, and one man sharpens another.
PROVERBS 27:17 ESV

For you were called to freedom, brothers. Only do not use your freedom as an opportunity for the flesh, but through love serve one another.
GALATIANS 5:13 ESV

Greeting One Another in Joy

Speaking to one another with psalms, hymns, and songs from the Spirit. Sing and make music from your heart to the Lord.

EPHESIANS 5:19 NIV

Want to try a fun experiment? The next time someone asks you how you're doing, instead of responding, "Okay," why not get more specific? Try "I'm blessed!" or "Having an awesome day!" Encourage yourself in the Lord and He will keep those spirits lifted. And encourage one another with words of blessing as well.

Dear Lord, I want to be a worthy friend. I want to show Your love to those around me in every way, and I want to be an example of joy to those around me. Fill my heart with joy so that I can share that joy with my friends. Help me to be trustworthy and wise in all of my dealings. Keep my spirits lifted so that I can raise the spirits of others. Amen.

Two are better than one, because they have a good reward for their toil. For if they fall, one will lift up his fellow. But woe to him who is alone when he falls and has not another to lift him up! Again, if two lie together, they keep warm, but how can one keep warm alone? And though a man might prevail against one who is alone, two will withstand him—a threefold cord is not quickly broken.

ECCLESIASTES 4:9–12 ESV

What is a friend? A single
soul dwelling in two bodies.

SAINT AUGUSTINE

Friendship is born at that moment when
one person says to another: What! You too?
I thought I was the only one.

C. S. LEWIS

Friendship is the source of the greatest pleasures,
and without friends even the most agreeable
pursuits become tedious.

THOMAS AQUINAS

*Do not rebuke an older man but encourage him as you would
a father, younger men as brothers, older women as mothers,
younger women as sisters, in all purity.*
I Timothy 5:1–2 ESV

*And let us consider one another in
order to stir up love and good works.*
Hebrews 10:24 NKJV

JOY *in Simplicity*

For our boast is this, the testimony of our conscience,
that we behaved in the world with simplicity and godly
sincerity, not by earthly wisdom but by the grace of God,
and supremely so toward you.

2 CORINTHIANS 1:12 ESV

Your world is not a simple one. New technology becomes obsolete by the next day, and people all around you are scrambling to get more stuff. "I want it! I need it!" might as well be the cry of the modern man. Does this seem empty to you? While there is a fleeting spark of happiness when you hold that new gadget in your hand or spin around in your new dress, this is not joy.

In 2 Corinthians, believers are called to "behave in the world with simplicity and godly sincerity." This does not mean that you need to adopt an ascetic lifestyle, but it is a reminder to be conscious of what you consume. True joy is found in relationships, nature, and the beauty of God's creation. Material things are just fleeting possessions that dull the senses.

If you base your happiness in worldly wealth, you will never feel complete. You can throw more and more merchandise into the hole in your heart, but that hole can only be filled with the joy of knowing God. Store up treasures in heaven, eschewing worldly excess. Instead of buying more and more things, spend some time outside enjoying the wonders of God's green earth. Read a book. Call a friend. Make some tea. Simplicity doesn't have to mean boring. You might be surprised at how happy you are when you let go of the world's standards.

And day by day, attending the temple together and breaking bread in their homes, they received their food with glad and generous hearts, praising God and having favor with all the people.

ACTS 2:46–47 ESV

For we are taking pains to do what is right, not only in the eyes of the Lord but also in the eyes of man.

2 CORINTHIANS 8:21 NIV

But seek first the kingdom of God and His righteousness, and all these things shall be added to you. Therefore do not worry about tomorrow, for tomorrow will worry about its own things. Sufficient for the day is its own trouble.

MATTHEW 6:33–34 NKJV

Joy is distinctly a Christian word and a Christian thing. It is the reverse of happiness. Happiness is the result of what happens of an agreeable sort. Joy has its springs deep down inside. And that spring never runs dry, no matter what happens. Only Jesus gives that joy. He had joy, singing its music within, even under the shadow of the cross.

S. D. GORDON

We ought to act with God in the greatest simplicity, speak to Him frankly and plainly, and implore His assistance in our affairs.

BROTHER LAWRENCE

I sometimes wonder whether all pleasures are not substitutes for joy.

C. S. LEWIS

Sing, O Heavens!

*Sing, O heavens; and be joyful, O earth; and break forth
into singing, O mountains: for the LORD hath comforted
his people, and will have mercy upon his afflicted.*

ISAIAH 49:13 KJV

Imagine you're walking through a meadow on
a dewy morning. The sweet smell of dawn lingers
in the air. Suddenly, like a skilled orchestra, the
heavens above begin to pour out an unexpected
song of joy. You close your eyes, overwhelmed by
the majesty of the moment. Scripture tells us the
heavens and the earth are joyful. . .so tune
in to their chorus today.

Dear Lord, thank You for Your beautiful creation! Nothing made by human hands can measure up to the majesty of the mountains, the delicacy of the lilac. Help me to be conscious of what You have done. I get so caught up in the rat race that I forget that material wealth is fleeting. Remind me of the pleasures of a simple life. My joy will be unmarred by the world. Amen.

"Do not lay up for yourselves treasures on earth, where moth and rust destroy and where thieves break in and steal; but lay up for yourselves treasures in heaven, where neither moth nor rust destroys and where thieves do not break in and steal. For where your treasure is, there your heart will be also."

MATTHEW 6:19–21 NKJV

"The lamp of the body is the eye. If therefore your eye is good, your whole body will be full of light."

MATTHEW 6:22 NKJV

If thou desire to profit, read with humility,
simplicity, and faithfulness; nor even
desire the repute of learning.

Thomas à Kempis

Purity and simplicity are the two wings with
which man soars above the earth and all temporary
nature. Simplicity is in the intention, purity in
the affection; simplicity turns to God; purity
unites with and enjoys him.

Thomas à Kempis

If we believe heaven to be our country, it is better
for us to transmit our wealth thither, than to retain
it here, where we may lose it by a sudden removal.

John Calvin

A Joy Forever

The Mighty One, God, the LORD, speaks and summons
the earth from the rising of the sun to where it sets.
From Zion, perfect in beauty, God shines forth.

PSALM 50:1–2 NIV

A child's face. A flowering pear tree. A rippling
brook. A mountain's peak. All of these things
overwhelm us with the magnitude of their beauty.
Why? Because we can see that they were created
by Someone much larger than ourselves, Someone
incredibly creative and colorful. We are reminded of
the awesomeness of God. Focus on the beauty He
has placed in your world. . .and praise Him!

Dear Lord, I am overwhelmed. You could have made the world boring and simply utilitarian, but instead You chose to fill the world with such beauty and majesty! I revel in Your creation, soaking in the light and color. It fills my heart with joy! Help me to realize that these are the things that matter. Worldly stuff is just dust. Creation and relationships: those are the things that bring true, unadulterated joy. Thank You for putting both into my path. Amen.

Better a little with the fear of the
LORD than great wealth with turmoil.
PROVERBS 15:16 NIV

Then Jesus said to his disciples, "Truly I tell you, it is hard for
someone who is rich to enter the kingdom of heaven. Again I
tell you, it is easier for a camel to go through the eye of a needle
than for someone who is rich to enter the kingdom of God."
MATTHEW 19:23–24 NIV

JOY *in Helping Others*

"He will reply, 'Truly I tell you, whatever you did not do for one of the least of these, you did not do for me.'"

*E*veryone likes it when good things happen to them. A healthy family and a fulfilling personal life are certainly causes for joy. However, do you really try to spread that joy? When you are in a time of plenty, do you ever think to share that with others?

People often have good intentions to help others. They plan to volunteer at soup kitchens, support a child overseas, or make meals for the family in their church that is going through a crisis. But life gets busy and helping others often falls by the wayside. It is easy to get wrapped up in your own life and forget about others. But imagine if

God had forgotten about you? Instead of ignoring your pleas, God chose to bless you beyond measure! Wouldn't it increase your joy to help bring joy to others?

You don't need lots of time or money to help others. Just taking a little time to help someone in need and to let them know that they are valued goes a long way. In Matthew 25 Jesus called His followers to reach out to "the least of these," or those in need. When you bring joy to others, you bring joy to Jesus. The greatest joy is definitely a joy that is shared! Don't cheat yourself or others out of an opportunity to be a part of this chain of joy!

"For there will never cease to be poor in the land. Therefore I command you, 'You shall open wide your hand to your brother, to the needy and to the poor, in your land.'"

DEUTERONOMY 15:11 ESV

What good is it, my brothers, if someone says he has faith but does not have works? Can that faith save him? If a brother or sister is poorly clothed and lacking in daily food, and one of you says to them, "Go in peace, be warmed and filled," without giving them the things needed for the body, what good is that? So also faith by itself, if it does not have works, is dead.

JAMES 2:14–17 ESV

"This is my commandment, that you love one another as I have loved you."

JOHN 15:12 ESV

The purpose of human life is to serve, and to show compassion and the will to help others.

ALBERT SCHWEITZER

What does love look like? It has the hands to help others. It has the feet to hasten to the poor and needy. It has eyes to see misery and want. It has the ears to hear the sighs and sorrows of men. That is what love looks like.

SAINT AUGUSTINE

You will find a joy in overcoming obstacles.

HELEN KELLER

A Life of Joy

*You have greatly encouraged me and
made me happy despite all our troubles.*
2 CORINTHIANS 7:4 NLT

Want to know the perfect recipe for happiness?
Spend your days focused on making others happy.
If you shift your focus from yourself to others, you
accomplish two things: you put others first, and you're
always looking for ways to make others smile. There's
something about spreading joy that satisfies the soul.

Dear Lord, I am a selfish being. Instead of caring about the well-being of my fellow man, I get wrapped up in my own desires and I forget about those around me who are hurting. What is joy worth if it isn't shared? Help me to act with compassion and to treat others with the dignity and care that they deserve. Just as You first loved me, help me to love others. Amen.

"Sell your possessions, and give to the needy. Provide yourselves with moneybags that do not grow old, with a treasure in the heavens that does not fail, where no thief approaches and no moth destroys. For where your treasure is, there will your heart be also."

LUKE 12:33–34 ESV

"Heal the sick, raise the dead, cleanse lepers, cast out demons. You received without paying; give without pay."

MATTHEW 10:8 ESV

"In the same way, let your light shine before others, so that they may see your good works and give glory to your Father who is in heaven."

MATTHEW 5:16 ESV

The first question which the priest and the Levite asked was: "If I stop to help this man, what will happen to me?" But the good Samaritan reversed the question: "If I do not stop to help this man, what will happen to him?"

MARTIN LUTHER KING JR.

God is the first object of our love: its next office is to bear the defects of others. And we should begin the practice of this amidst our own household.

JOHN WESLEY

Compassion is sometimes the fatal capacity for feeling what it is like to live inside somebody else's skin. It is the knowledge that there can never really be any peace and joy for me until there is peace and joy finally for you too.

FREDERICK BUECHNER

A Net of Love

No one has ever seen God; but if we love one another,
God lives in us and his love is made complete in us.

1 JOHN 4:12 NIV

It's hard to be a good witness if you've got a sour expression on your face. People aren't usually won to the Lord by grumpy friends and coworkers. If you hope to persuade people that life in Jesus is the ultimate, then you've got to let your enthusiasm shine through. Before you reach for the net, spend some time on your knees, asking for an infusion of joy. Then go catch some fish!

Dear Lord, it has been said that "they will know that we are Christians by our love." I am ashamed to say that this is not always the case regarding me. I do not love others in the manner that befits a believer. I have been loved by You, and that makes me glad! Let the knowledge of Your love move me to love others in an intentional way. Make me a messenger of joy! Amen.

Bear one another's burdens,
and so fulfill the law of Christ.
GALATIANS 6:2 ESV

We love because he first loved us. If anyone says,
"I love God," and hates his brother, he is a liar; for he who
does not love his brother whom he has seen cannot love
God whom he has not seen. And this commandment we have
from him: whoever loves God must also love his brother.
1 JOHN 4:19–21 ESV

Contribute to the needs of the
saints and seek to show hospitality.
ROMANS 12:13 ESV

JOY *in Hard Work*

I can do all things through
him who strengthens me.
PHILIPPIANS 4:13 ESV

There are few things as satisfying as a job well done. Whether you finish a project at work or maintain a clean household, it is nice to be able to step back and realize that you did a job well. It is good to have a sense of purpose in your day. Sometimes in your busiest moments, you may daydream about living a life of idleness where you watch movies and eat chocolate all day, but where is the true joy in that? What would you be achieving in that? Absolutely nothing. While it may seem appealing in times of weakness, it would ultimately only lead to boredom and unhappiness.

Finding a calling in the day to day is one of the greatest joys on earth. People are commanded to be stewards of the earth, and this can only be done through hard work. This is not to say that work is always fulfilling. Sometimes work is overwhelming or feels insignificant, and it is easy to get discouraged. How do you find joy in these times?

It says in Philippians 4 that "I can do all things through him who strengthens me." Not just the easy things, *all* things. What a blessed reminder of God's faithfulness to His people! Knowing that the Lord is on your side at all times is such a cause for joy! In order to honor God and those around you, give every project your best effort. This will bring glory to God and increase your satisfaction.

Whatever you do, work heartily,
as for the Lord and not for men.

COLOSSIANS 3:23 ESV

Do all things without grumbling or disputing, that you
may be blameless and innocent, children of God without
blemish in the midst of a crooked and twisted generation,
among whom you shine as lights in the world.

PHILIPPIANS 2:14–15 ESV

The soul of the sluggard craves and gets nothing,
while the soul of the diligent is richly supplied.

PROVERBS 13:4 ESV

The reflections on a day well spent furnish us with
joys more pleasing than ten thousand triumphs.

THOMAS À KEMPIS

Pray as though everything depended on God.
Work as though everything depended on you.

SAINT AUGUSTINE

If God is satisfied with the work,
the work may be satisfied with itself.

C. S. LEWIS

Have thy tools ready. God will find thee work.

CHARLES KINGSLEY

The Fork in the Road

*What do people get for all the toil and anxious
striving with which they labor under the sun?*

ECCLESIASTES 2:22 NIV

Imagine you're approaching a fork in the road.
You're unsure of which way to turn. If you knew
ahead of time that the road to the right would be
filled with joy and the road to the left would lead
to sorrow, wouldn't it make the decision easier?
Today, as you face multiple decisions, ask God
to lead you down the right road.

Dear Lord, help me fight off the hard grip of laziness. Show me the value in treating every task at hand as an opportunity to praise You with my work. You did not create people to be idle. Lead me down the right path, the path to joy, even if it is the more difficult path. Thank You for entrusting me with a job to do. I pray that I do it well. Amen.

*So, whether you eat or drink, or whatever
you do, do all to the glory of God.*
1 Corinthians 10:31 esv

*Whatever your hand finds to do,
do it with your might.*
Ecclesiastes 9:10 esv

*And whatever you do, in word or deed,
do everything in the name of the Lord Jesus,
giving thanks to God the Father through him.*
Colossians 3:17 esv

*The Lord God took the man and put him
in the garden of Eden to work it and keep it.*
Genesis 2:15 esv

There is no work, however vile or sordid,
that does not glisten before God.

JOHN CALVIN

Temptations which accompany the working day
will be conquered on the basis of the morning
breakthrough to God. Decisions, demanded by
work, become easier and simpler where they are
made not in the fear of man, but only in the sight
of God. He wants to give us today the power
which we need for our work.

DIETRICH BONHOEFFER

Deprived of meaningful work,
men and women lose their reason for
existence; they go stark, raving mad.

FYODOR DOSTOYEVSKY

The Fruit of Your Labor

You will eat the fruit of your labor;
blessings and prosperity will be yours.
PSALM 128:2 NIV

We're always waiting for the payoff, aren't we?
When we've put a lot of effort into a project,
for example, we hope to see good results. The Word
of God promises that we will eat the fruit of our
labor—that we will eventually experience blessings
and prosperity. So all of that hard work will be
worth it. But remember, the joy is in the journey!
It's not just in the payoff.

Dear Lord, make me patient. Often I only work for the payoff, instead of the satisfaction that can come from the process. Help me to take joy in my work, not just in the fruits of my labor. Help me to approach every task, no matter how small, with joyful vigor. If You can take the time to paint color on every flower, I can take the time to do a job well! Amen.

Look carefully then how you walk, not as unwise but as wise,
making the best use of the time, because the days are evil.
Ephesians 5:15–16 esv

Let the thief no longer steal, but rather let him labor,
doing honest work with his own hands, so that he may
have something to share with anyone in need.
Ephesians 4:28 esv

Unless the Lord builds the house, those who build it
labor in vain. Unless the Lord watches over the city,
the watchman stays awake in vain.
Psalm 127:1 esv

JOY *in Pain*

May those who sow in tears reap with shouts of joy!
He that goes forth weeping, bearing the seed for sowing, shall
come home with shouts of joy, bringing his sheaves with him.

PSALM 126:5–6 RSV

*L*iving a life in faithfulness to God does not promise smooth sailing. Pain comes knocking around every turn. The devil lurks in the shadows to find ways to bring the believer down into the bog of emptiness and despair. If you can't even keep from crying, how is it possible to live a life of joy?

The psalmists (usually King David) understand the pain that can accompany the life of the believer. The vivid wording reveals a heart in turmoil: tears, weeping, wailing. These are not the words of a heart at peace. However, they are quick to add that joy follows after! You follow a faithful God, and He will not abandon you to your suffering. You may sow in tears, but you will reap with shouts of joy!

The apostle Paul is also an excellent example of living a life of joy despite extreme pain. Beaten, persecuted, and jailed for his devotion to the cause of the Gospel, Paul's letters still brim over with words of peace and joy! The reason for that is this: God does not use "whole" people. He does great things with the broken ones. To truly be able to rejoice in the salvation of God, you have to be brought low so that He can build you up as something new. Instead of being crippled by grief and fear, approach the throne of the King. He will bind up your broken heart and replace it with a heart of joy.

"Very truly I tell you, you will weep and mourn while the world rejoices. You will grieve, but your grief will turn to joy."
JOHN 16:20 NIV

"Do not grieve, for the joy of the LORD is your strength."
NEHEMIAH 8:10 NIV

Count it all joy, my brothers, when you meet trials of various kinds, for you know that the testing of your faith produces steadfastness. And let steadfastness have its full effect, that you may be perfect and complete, lacking in nothing.
JAMES 1:2–4 ESV

You must submit to supreme suffering in
order to discover the completion of joy.

JOHN CALVIN

You must be made miserable before you can
know true Christian joy. Indeed the real trouble
with the miserable Christian is that he has never
been truly made miserable because of conviction
of sin. He has bypassed the essential preliminary
to joy, he has been assuming something that
he has no right to assume.

MARTYN LLOYD-JONES

We could never learn to be brave and patient,
if there were only joy in the world.

HELEN KELLER

A Compassionate Heart

Break forth into joy, sing together, you waste
places of Jerusalem! For the LORD has comforted
His people, He has redeemed Jerusalem.
ISAIAH 52:9 NKJV

Have you ever knelt to comfort a child as the tears
flowed down his or her little cheeks? If so, then
you understand the heart of your Daddy God as
He gently wipes away your tears during times of
sorrow. He comforts as only a Father can, bringing
hope where there is no hope and joy where there is
no joy. What a compassionate God we serve!

Dear Lord, I am broken. The world is too much for me to face alone. I am overwhelmed by the darkness. Do not abandon me to despair. I call out to You for help. Please hear my prayer. Help me to be joyful in all things, even the things that hurt. Help me to be a light for You in dark places. I cannot let my joy be contingent upon my surroundings. Thank You for hearing my earnest plea. Amen.

"Peace I leave with you; my peace I give to you.
Not as the world gives do I give to you. Let not
your hearts be troubled, neither let them be afraid."

JOHN 14:27 ESV

But he said to me, "My grace is sufficient for you,
for my power is made perfect in weakness." Therefore I
will boast all the more gladly of my weaknesses, so that the
power of Christ may rest upon me. For the sake of Christ, then,
I am content with weaknesses, insults, hardships, persecutions,
and calamities. For when I am weak, then I am strong.

2 CORINTHIANS 12:9–10 ESV

Now I rejoice in my sufferings for your sake, and in
my flesh I am filling up what is lacking in Christ's
afflictions for the sake of his body, that is, the church.

COLOSSIANS 1:24 ESV

There is no virtue in the Christian life which was not made to radiate with joy; there is no circumstance and no occasion which is not illuminated with joy. A joyless life is not a Christian life, for joy is one constant recipe for Christian living.

WILLIAM BARCLAY

We rejoice in spite of our grief,
not in place of it.

WOODROW KROLL

Do you want comfort? Nothing can give it so much as the thought of His coming. There may be sorrow in the night, but joy enough—fullness of joy—in that morning when we shall see Him as He is: fullness of joy in being like Him and with Him forevermore.

G. V. WIGRAM

Partakers of Joy

But rejoice inasmuch as you participate
in the sufferings of Christ, so that you
may be overjoyed when his glory is revealed.
I PETER 4:13 NIV

Ever feel like you've signed on for the suffering
but not the joy? We are called to be partakers in
Christ's sufferings. We wouldn't really know Him
if we didn't walk in the valleys occasionally. But,
praise God! We are also partakers in His glorious
resurrection. We have the power of the cross to
spur us on! The time has come to trade in those
sorrows. Reach for His unspeakable joy.

Dear Lord, I feel so alone. I feel abandoned by those around me, but I know in my heart that You will never abandon me. Fill my heart with joy in the midst of sorrow, so that I may spread that joy to others who are also in pain. Remind me that You are the God of hope, even when I seem to have lost my hope. You will never abandon me, even when all seems dark. Amen.

May the God of hope fill you with all joy and
peace in believing, so that by the power of the
Holy Spirit you may abound in hope.

ROMANS 15:13 ESV

For I consider that the sufferings of this present time are not
worth comparing with the glory that is to be revealed to us.
For the creation waits with eager longing for the revealing of
the sons of God. For the creation was subjected to futility, not
willingly, but because of him who subjected it, in hope that the
creation itself will be set free from its bondage to corruption
and obtain the freedom of the glory of the children of God.

ROMANS 8:18–21 ESV

JOY *in Temptation*

When I said, "My foot is slipping," your unfailing love,
Lᴏʀᴅ, supported me. When anxiety was great within me,
your consolation brought me joy.
Pꜱᴀʟᴍ 94:18–19 ɴɪᴠ

𝒥n a world saturated with lust, permissiveness, and carnality, it can seem "uncool" to cling to the promises of God. Wouldn't it be so much easier to give in to temptation? The devil is so crafty that oftentimes it doesn't even feel like giving in to temptation; it's just living your life. However, this is a lie. By giving in to temptation, you are cheating yourself out of the joy of a godly life! However, it is impossible to resist on your own.

It is said that God does not give you more than you can handle, but in order to resist, you have to abide in God. Read His Word. Pray daily. Seek counsel from other believers. If your feet are strong on the path of righteousness, nothing is too hard for God! You will come to realize that the worldly things that you used to desire are fleeting and shallow. Why would anyone trade in the joy that comes from serving God for something so hollow?

It is easy to say "how simple to resist" until the moment of temptation actually arrives. It can be so hard to resist. In the moment, remind yourself of God's promises to never abandon you. Knowing that you are not alone in the struggle is a great source of joy. You have a loving and faithful Father! Rejoice in Him today!

The prospect of the righteous is joy,
but the hopes of the wicked come to nothing.
PROVERBS 10:28 NIV

No temptation has overtaken you except what is common
to mankind. And God is faithful; he will not let you be
tempted beyond what you can bear. But when you are tempted,
he will also provide a way out so that you can endure it.
1 CORINTHIANS 10:13 NIV

My brethren, count it all joy when you fall into various trials,
knowing that the testing of your faith produces patience.
JAMES 1:2–3 NKJV

The joy of the Lord will arm us against the
assault of our spiritual enemies and put our
mouths out of taste for those pleasures with
which the tempter baits his hooks.

MATTHEW HENRY

Man cannot live without joy; therefore when he
is deprived of true spiritual joys it is necessary
that he become addicted to carnal pleasures.

THOMAS AQUINAS

A Joyous Crown

Blessed is the one who perseveres under trial because,
having stood the test, that person will receive the crown
of life that the Lord has promised to those who love him.

JAMES 1:12 NIV

We are so focused on the joys of this life that we
sometimes forget the exquisite joys yet to come
in the next. Enduring and overcoming temptation
can bring us great satisfaction here on earth, but
imagine the crown of life we're one day going to
receive. Nothing can compare! Oh, the joy of
eternal life. Oh, the thrill of that joyous crown.

Dear Lord, thank You for Your promises of heaven! Knowing that there are treasures stored up for me in heaven makes enduring constant temptation satisfying. Keep my feet steady on Your path; I may glance from side to side, but I will remain strong in Your Word. I know that You do not give me more than I can handle. Amen.

"Watch and pray that you may not enter into temptation.
The spirit indeed is willing, but the flesh is weak."
MATTHEW 26:41 ESV

Prove me, O LORD, and try me;
test my heart and my mind.
PSALM 26:2 ESV

"I the LORD search the heart and test the mind, to give every
man according to his ways, according to the fruit of his deeds."
JEREMIAH 17:10 ESV

When Christians find themselves exposed to temptation they should pray to God to uphold them, and when they are tempted they should not be discouraged. It is not a sin to be tempted; the sin is to fall into temptation.

D. L. MOODY

We usually know what we can do,
but temptation shows us who we are.

THOMAS À KEMPIS

It is a common temptation of Satan to make us give up the reading of the Word and prayer when our enjoyment is gone; as if it were of no use to read the Scriptures when we do not enjoy them, and as if it were no use to pray when we have no spirit of prayer.

GEORGE MÜLLER

Rooted and Grounded

"Those on the rocky ground are the ones who receive the word with joy when they hear it, but they have no root. They believe for a while, but in the time of testing they fall away."

LUKE 8:13 NIV

Imagine a sturdy oak tree, one that's been growing for decades. Its roots run deep. It's grounded. When the storms of life strike, that tree is going to stand strong. Now think of your own roots. Do they run deep? When temptations strike, will you stand strong? Dig into the Word. Receive it with joy. Let it be your foundation. Plant yourself and let your roots run deep.

Dear Lord, I am anxious. I feel the temptations of the world, the flesh, and the devil hard at my door and often feel powerless against them. I am weak, but You are strong. Help me to stand strong on Your promises and to put on the armor of God. You are my strength and my joy. Even when trials seem too much to bear, I know that You are with me. Amen.

Submit yourselves, then, to God.
Resist the devil, and he will flee from you.
JAMES 4:7 NIV

Be alert and of sober mind. Your enemy the devil prowls
around like a roaring lion looking for someone to devour.
I PETER 5:8 NIV

Put on the full armor of God, so that you can
take your stand against the devil's schemes.
EPHESIANS 6:11 NIV

JOY *in Practice*

*Therefore if you have any encouragement from being united
with Christ, if any comfort from his love, if any common
sharing in the Spirit, if any tenderness and compassion,
then make my joy complete by being like-minded, having
the same love, being one in spirit and of one mind.*

PHILIPPIANS 2:1–2 NIV

*J*oy is not something that comes naturally to
everyone. While some people are just naturally
optimistic and happy, for most, it takes practice.
It is so easy to get weighed down by circumstance.
You ask yourself, "How can I be joyful if there is
so much suffering around me? How can I even be
joyful with all the small things going wrong in my
every day?" As with every other spiritual trait, joy
takes work.

Living a joyful life requires being very intentional and being determined. Having joy means
looking at the world around you and saying,

"Things may be hard, but I am loved by God, and for that I am glad."

Being intentional in your joy does not mean putting on a shiny, happy face and being perky every second of every day. Joy does not minimize the pain and frustration of life, but instead is a recognition that even when things are hard, God has given us a reason to rejoice in the promise of salvation and the hope of heaven. Even when circumstances seem to squelch your joy, knowing that God is in control is a comfort. Knowing that you are not alone in this fight can change your perspective significantly. You have the God of the universe in your corner, and that is cause for joy!

We are to be re-made. All the rabbit in
us is to disappear—and then, surprisingly,
we shall find underneath it all a thing
we have never yet imagined: a real Man,
an ageless god, a son of God, strong, radiant,
wise, beautiful, and drenched in joy.

C. S. LEWIS

Do not let the empty cup be your first teacher
of the blessings you had when it was full.
Do not let a bad place here and there in the
bed destroy your rest. Seek, as a plain duty,
to cultivate a buoyant, joyous sense of the
crowded kindnesses of God in your daily life.

ALEXANDER MACLAREN

Dear Lord, I fail so often to put my joy into practice. I read Your Word, and I understand in my head that I need to be joyful no matter my circumstances, and yet I am still afraid and still bitter. Remind me of Your promises, Lord. Remind me that You have saved me from the pain of sin and death, and that alone is cause to rejoice! Make my contrite heart rejoice. Amen.

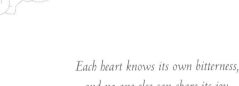

Each heart knows its own bitterness,
and no one else can share its joy.

PROVERBS 14:10 NIV

Though you have not seen him, you love him. Though you
do not now see him, you believe in him and rejoice with
joy that is inexpressable and filled with glory, the outcome
of your faith, obtaining the salvation of your souls.

I PETER 1:8–9 ESV

The whole earth is filled with awe at your wonders;
where morning dawns, where evening fades,
you call forth songs of joy.

PSALM 65:8 NIV

Your success and happiness lie in you. Resolve
to keep happy, and your joy and you shall
form an invincible host against difficulties.

HELEN KELLER

To pursue joy is to lose it. The only way to get
it is to follow steadily the path of duty, without
thinking of joy, and then, like sheep, it comes most
surely unsought, and we "being in the way," the
angel of God, bright-haired joy, is sure to meet us.

ALEXANDER MACLAREN

No one can get joy by merely asking for it.
It is one of the ripest fruits of the Christian life,
and, like all fruits, must be grown.

HENRY DRUMMOND

The Joy of His Heart

For he shall not much remember the days of his life;
because God answereth him in the joy of his heart.

ECCLESIASTES 5:20 KJV

Sometimes we go through things that we wish we
could forget. Hard things. Hurtful things. But God,
in His remarkable way, eases the pain of our bumps
in the road, and before long, we can barely remember
them. Joy rises up in place of pain, and we move
forward, content in the fact that tomorrow will be
better than yesterday. Don't focus on yesterday.
Live for today and look forward to tomorrow.

Dear Lord, my heart is overflowing with praise! You have saved me, and I am glad! You have given me so many reasons to rejoice—how could I do otherwise? You provide for my needs, shelter me and my family from harm, and promise eternal life in heaven. I am looking ahead to a brighter tomorrow while I make the best of what I have been given today. You are forever gracious. Amen.

Being strengthened with all power according to
his glorious might so that you may have great
endurance and patience, and giving joyful thanks
to the Father, who has qualified you to share in the
inheritance of his holy people in the kingdom of light.
COLOSSIANS 1:11–12 NIV

Now may the God of hope fill you with all
joy and peace in believing, that you may abound
in hope by the power of the Holy Spirit.
ROMANS 15:13 NKJV